NBA
All-Star
Allen Iverson

by **John Hareas**

SCHOLASTIC INC.

New York   Toronto   London   Auckland   Sydney
Mexico City   New Delhi   Hong Kong   Buenos Aires

To my All-Star readers, Emma and Christopher.

ISBN 0-439-44301-6

12 11 10 9 8 7 6 5 4 3 2 1   3 4 5 6 7/0

Printed in the U.S.A.
First Scholastic printing, November 2003
Book Design: Louise Bova

Contents

The Answer

Allen Iverson is one of the most exciting players in the NBA. He is 6 feet tall and weighs 160 pounds, which is small for an NBA player. But he has super-sized skills. He is one of the NBA's top scorers. He uses his speed to dribble past opponents and score. Every play of his is

• Allen and his mom have some fun together at a game.

amazing! Allen is a giant talent — but he also has a giant heart.

"I don't play with my size," said Allen. "I just play with my heart."

Allen also has a big heart off the court. He visits hospitals and

• Allen dishes assists in the community, too!

spends time with sick children. He also started the Cross Over Foundation. It hosts a charity basketball game in his hometown that raises money for children from poor neighborhoods. It's important for Allen to help out. He once lived in a poor neighborhood, too.

Allen had a tough childhood. But he grew up to

become one of the best basketball players in the world. Allen became a superstar. But he stayed true to himself and to his family and childhood friends. He dresses the way he wants to. He acts the way he wants to. He is his own person.

"I'm just trying to be me," Allen has said.

Allen entered the NBA in 1996. He made a big splash. They nicknamed him "The Answer." Allen played well and was named the Rookie of the Year. That season, he scored

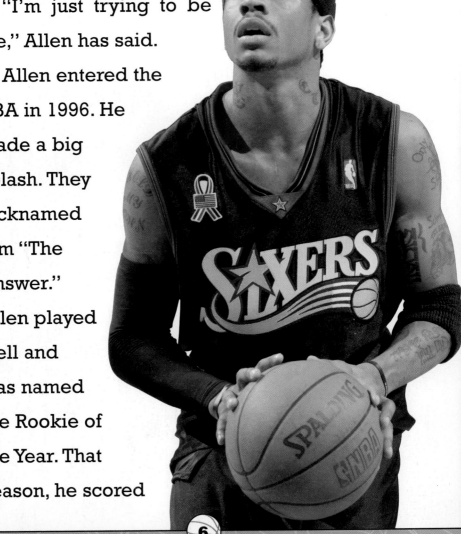

40 or more points five games in a row. It was a rookie record!

That was just the beginning. Allen made All-Star teams and won scoring titles. He even won the NBA's Most Valuable Player Award. He also helped lead his team, the Philadelphia 76ers, to the NBA Finals. He plays hard. He plays when he is hurt. Allen just never quits. He gives it his all, all the time.

Did You Know?
Philadelphia is
Allen's favorite city.

Humble Beginnings

Allen Ezail Iverson was born on June 7, 1975. His mother, Ann, knew he was special as soon as she saw him. She also knew he would be a basketball player. He was 22 inches long when he was born. That's one tall baby!

Allen grew up in Hampton, Virginia. He lived with his mother and his grandmother. Their house was on Jordan Drive. The street had the same name as one of Allen's all-time favorite basketball players: Michael Jordan.

• Allen's youth basketball team. He is in the second row, wearing #12.

When Allen was five, he and his mother left his grandmother's house. They moved to Newport News, Virginia. They lived in a project called Stewart Garden Apartments. It was a poor and violent area. A lot of people got in trouble for doing things they weren't supposed to be doing. But Allen liked where he lived. He made a lot of friends there. He is still friends with many of them today. Some of his friends got in trouble, too. But Allen chose a different path. He and his friends played *a lot* of sports. They played basketball. But they also played football and baseball.

At first, Allen didn't like basketball very much. But his mother made him play. He didn't have a choice.

"I came home one day," said Allen, "and my mom said, 'Today, you're going to basketball practice.'" Allen cried all the way out the door.

When he got to practice, Allen was surprised. He really liked basketball. In fact, he

• Allen's No. 1 Supporter—his mom!

couldn't wait to play again. He has been playing ever since.

Allen lived with his mother and his baby sister, Brandy. The family didn't have very much money. Sometimes, their apartment didn't have lights or water. But his mom always told Allen that he could

• The Allen Iverson Day parade, 1996.

be anything he wanted to be. And he believed her. Some of his friends got in trouble a lot. But Allen tried hard to stay out of trouble. He thought about his future.

Allen wanted to help his family. He decided that he would make it into the NBA. The odds were one in a million. But Allen knew he had to reach his dream.

Did You Know?
In his free time, Allen likes to draw.

High School and College Star

Allen went to Bethel High School. It was his mother's high school when she was young. Allen was great at football and basketball. Many people thought that football was his best sport, not basketball!

Allen was an instant star. He played on the varsity football team as a freshman. The next year, he was the team's quarterback and safety. His team never lost a game! In his junior year, Allen had a dream sea-

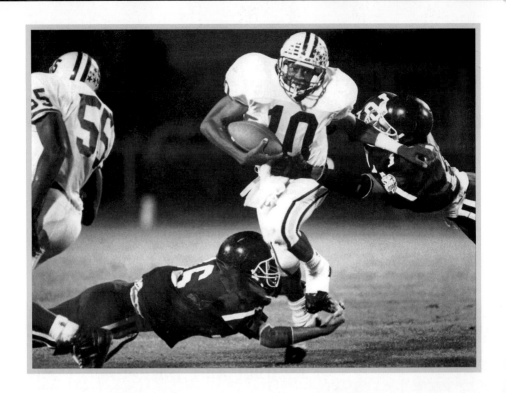

son. He passed for 14 touchdowns, scored 21 touchdowns and had eight interceptions. Allen broke a Virginia high school record. He was named Player of the Year.

That season, Allen led his team to the Virginia State championship. In the title game, Allen scored two touchdowns, threw for two more and picked off two interceptions. But that wasn't enough for Allen. He wanted to win the state basketball title, too.

Allen traded in his cleats for his basketball sneakers. He had a great season on the court, too. Allen averaged 31.6 points per game. He thrilled crowds with his quickness and all-around skills. And at the end of the season, Allen's team won the state basketball title.

Allen was named Virginia's high school basketball *and* football Player of the Year. He was on a roll.

Then his good luck ran out. One night Allen went bowling with his friends. A fight broke out. When the police came, they thought it was Allen's fault. As a result, he spent time in jail.

"I was in the wrong place at the wrong time," Allen said. Eventually, the courts decided he was innocent. Allen got to go home.

He did not stay home for long. Soon it was time to go to college.

Allen could have played football or basketball in college. He picked basketball. He still dreamed of making it into the NBA. Allen went to Georgetown University in Washington, D.C. Allen's coach, John Thompson, was like a father to Allen. He helped Allen on and off the court.

Allen was a star at Georgetown, too. He averaged 20.4 points and 4.5 assists in his freshman season. His second season, he averaged 25 points and 4.7 assists. He was named First Team All-American.

But Allen wasn't happy. Whenever he went home to see his family, he saw how hard their life was. After his sophomore season, he got tired of waiting. It was time to go after his dream. He was going to the NBA.

Did You Know?

When Allen's mother was in high school, she was on the girls' basketball team.

Hello, Philadelphia

The Philadelphia 76ers finished the 1995–96 season with a 18–64 record. They had the third worst record in the NBA that season. Twelve other teams also finished with poor records. Those teams, along with the Sixers, were in a lottery. The bounce of the Ping-Pong balls would decide which team got the first pick in the 1996 NBA Draft. Pat Croce, former president of the Sixers, knew who he would pick if he got the chance: Allen Iverson.

The Ping-Pong balls bounced Philadelphia's way. The Sixers won the first pick.

Philadelphia has a history of great NBA players.

• He's No. 1! NBA Commissioner David Stern welcomes Allen to the NBA.

Superstars Paul Arizin, Wilt Chamberlain, Billy Cunningham, Julius Erving, Moses Malone and Charles Barkley all played for the Sixers. Philly fans wanted another star player. They thought Allen would lead their team to glory. So when the Sixers got the first draft pick, they picked Allen. Allen's NBA dream finally came true!

Before the draft, Allen was nervous. He thought

he would be picked, but he wasn't sure who would pick him. When he heard his name called out, he was very excited. He was finally in the NBA!

Allen didn't disappoint the Philadelphia fans. He didn't play like a rookie. He played like a star! The fans soon saw why he was the number one pick. No one could stop his quick moves to the basket or his quick shooting release. He also faked out his opponents with his crossover dribble. Allen would dribble one way and then in an instant, dribble the opposite way.

Some players are very good at handling the ball. Some players are very fast. Allen was both. And that made him special. He scored lots of points.

Allen was a very confident player. He was fearless on the basketball court. One day, Allen finally played against Michael Jordan, his childhood hero. Fans filled the Philadelphia arena. The game was sold out. Allen used his crossover move on Michael and he scored! The crowd cheered wildly.

Allen had a great first season. He scored 40 points or more for five consecutive games. It was a new rookie record! Allen broke the old record set by Hall of Famer Wilt Chamberlain. He averaged 23.5 points and 7.1 assists that season. He was also a good defender. He averaged two steals

a game. Allen's all-around game earned him Rookie of the Year honors! But even though Allen played great, his team still had a losing season. They won 22 games and lost 60. Adding Allen to the team hadn't been enough. Something else would have to change.

Allen wasn't always popular with the fans. When he played his idol, Michael Jordan, Allen did not back down. He stood up to Michael on the court. Some people thought that he did not give Michael enough respect. They got mad at Allen. It hurt his reputation.

Did You Know?
Allen's favorite foods are lasagna and fried shrimp.

The Long Climb

After Allen's rookie season, the Sixers hired a new head coach, Larry Brown. He was one of basketball's most successful coaches — he knew how to win. Brown won a national championship at Kansas. His teams had won more than 850 games at the NBA and ABA levels. He and Allen were both stars. But they were very different. Pat Croce used to be president of the Sixers. He said that when Allen and Brown got together "it was like when the worlds collide."

Brown wanted Allen to play within the team. Allen wanted to run the

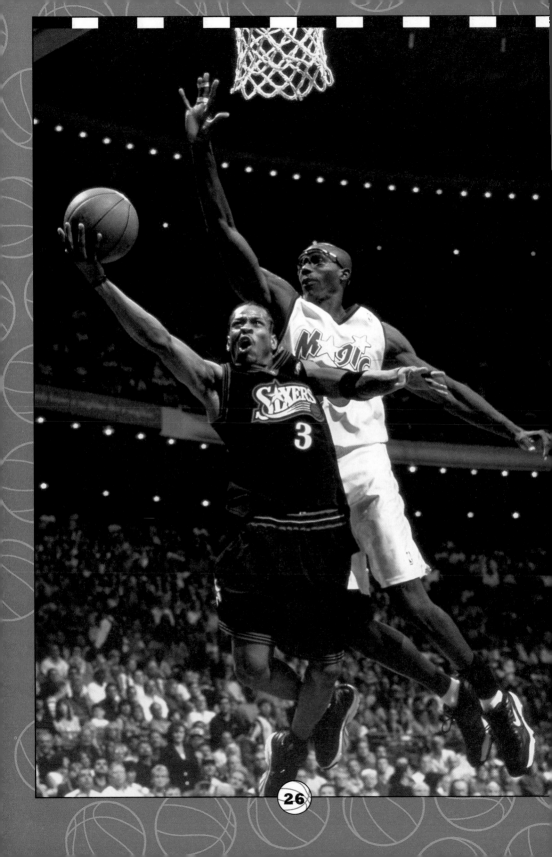

• Allen talks strategy with former Coach Larry Brown.

team his way. They disagreed with each other, but they both wanted the same result: victory.

Brown led the team in the right direction. In his first season, the Sixers had a 31–51 record. They won 13 more games that year than they had the year before. Fans knew something special was happening.

The next season, Brown made a change. Allen no longer would play point guard. Brown switched

Did You Know?

Allen likes to help people. He started the Cross Over Foundation and he hosts the annual Allen Iverson Celebrity Classic.

Allen's position to shooting guard. Allen was such a great scorer that he would be able to score more points at that position. The move paid off.

"I could see a change," said Brown. "A change for the better."

The Sixers were now Allen's team. Brown built the Sixers around him. Brown traded many of the Sixers players. He kept Allen. The Sixers had all new players to help out Allen, their scoring machine. Suddenly, the Sixers started to win. They made the playoffs for the first time in eight years!

Allen had a great season at his new position. He averaged 26.7 points a game, the best in the NBA! He also received another great honor. Allen made the All-NBA First Team. Everything was falling in place.

The Sixers played the Orlando Magic in the playoffs. Allen helped the underdog Sixers defeat the Magic in four games. He even had nine steals in one game — an NBA Playoff record! Next, the Sixers played the Indiana Pacers. The Pacers were too much for the Sixers. Indiana won in four games.

But even though the Sixers lost, the team was clearly on the right track.

The Turning Point

Allen's star continued to shine in the next season, 1999–2000. Allen made the NBA All-Star team for the first time. It meant a lot to him, because he had always watched the All-Star Game when he was a kid. He had always wanted to be an All-Star. And now he was!

"It was like a dream come true," said Allen. He knew he would remember that feeling for the rest of his life.

Allen was one of the NBA's best players. Teams tried to stop him from scoring but couldn't. He was too good and too quick.

But not everyone accepted Allen. He dressed differently from other players. He had a lot of tattoos and a cornrow hairstyle. He was just being himself. But not everyone liked Allen the way he was. They thought he should dress and act like other NBA stars. But Allen disagreed.

"I don't want to be Michael Jordan," he said. "I don't want to be Magic [Johnson] or [Larry] Bird or Isiah [Thomas]." Allen just wanted to be himself. "I want to be able to look in the mirror and say I did it my way."

So Allen did it his way.

When the Sixers lost to

the Pacers in the playoffs again, there were questions about Allen's future in Philadelphia.

Allen was almost traded to a different team. He was sad, because he didn't want to leave Philadelphia. And he didn't want to leave the Sixers.

"I always wanted to be a Sixer," said Allen. "I wanted to start my career as a Sixer and end my career as a Sixer."

In the end, Allen wasn't traded. He got to stay in the city he loves.

Allen was 25 years old. He decided it was time to change his life.

Did You Know?

Allen won the NBA's scoring title three times out of four seasons (1998-99, 2000-01, 2001-02)

MVP! MVP! MVP!

A llen started the next season with a new attitude. He was named team captain. Now he wasn't just a player, he was a leader. Philadelphia had a great season, thanks to their new captain. They won their first 10 games. That season, the Sixers had the best record in the Eastern Conference, 56–26.

It was a great season for Allen, too. He won the 2001 All-Star Game MVP. The game was played in Washington, D.C., the same city where he played college basketball. When he got the MVP trophy, Allen asked for his coach. The award, he said, was a tribute to Coach Brown, and to his family and his friends.

Allen grew as a player and as a person. And it showed. He gained more and more fans. People

respected the way he was true to himself and his team.

That season, Allen was the NBA's MVP. He averaged 31.1 points per game and added another scoring title to his collection. The Sixers played the Pacers in the playoffs again. But this time, they won!

Allen and the Sixers met Vince Carter and the

Toronto Raptors in the Eastern Conference Semi-finals. It was a record-breaking game. In Game 2, Allen scored 54 points. In the fourth quarter, he scored 19 points in a row! Vince responded and scored 50 in Game 3. They made NBA history. It was the first time two players on competing teams

scored 50 or more points in one game after another! That wasn't enough for Allen. He also scored 52 points in Game 5!

Allen and the Sixers beat the Raptors in seven thrilling games. Then they played the Milwaukee Bucks. The Sixers beat them, too. Allen scored 44 points in Game 7 of that series. The Sixers became the Eastern Conference champions! Allen had waited five long years for this chance. Now he was taking the Sixers to the NBA Finals. They would face the defending NBA champions, the Los Angeles Lakers!

• Allen shows off his All-Star Game MVP trophy.

The Lakers were led by two superstars, Shaquille O'Neal and Kobe Bryant. Everyone thought they would win. L.A. was undefeated in the 2001 playoffs. Not many people thought Philadelphia had a chance.

But in Game 1, the Sixers shocked the world. They beat the Lakers on their home court! The Sixers won Game 1 in overtime 107–101. Allen scored 48 points. The Sixers had done better than anyone expected. But it wasn't good enough. L.A. won the next four games. The Lakers won their second NBA title.

Allen was sad that the Sixers didn't win the championship. But it was still a great season for Allen, on and off the court. He was a great player and a great leader. He was proud of himself, no matter what. By working hard and playing hard, this fearless leader made his dream come true!

Did You Know?

Allen was named MVP of the 1997 Rookie Game in Cleveland.

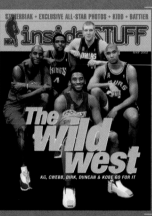